PIONEER VALLEY EDUCATIONAL

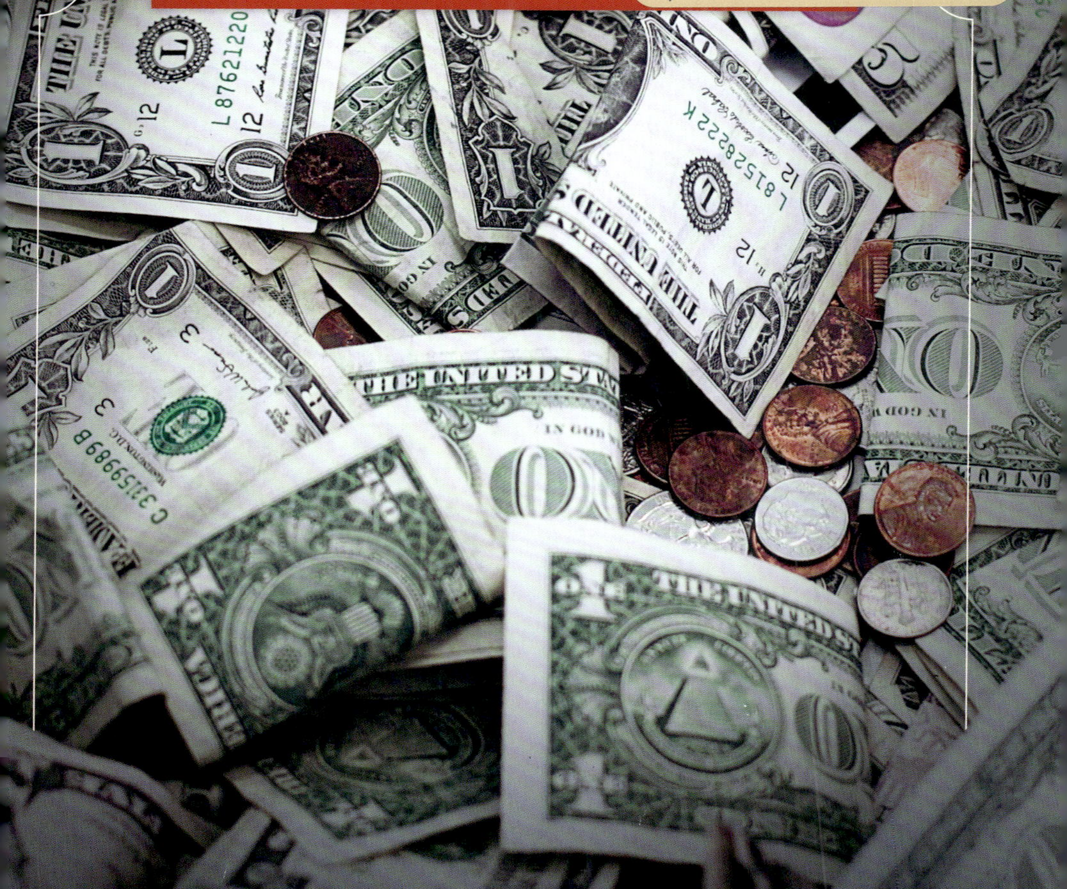

DOLLARS AND CENTS

MICHÈLE DUFRESNE

Here is a penny.
A penny is 1 cent.

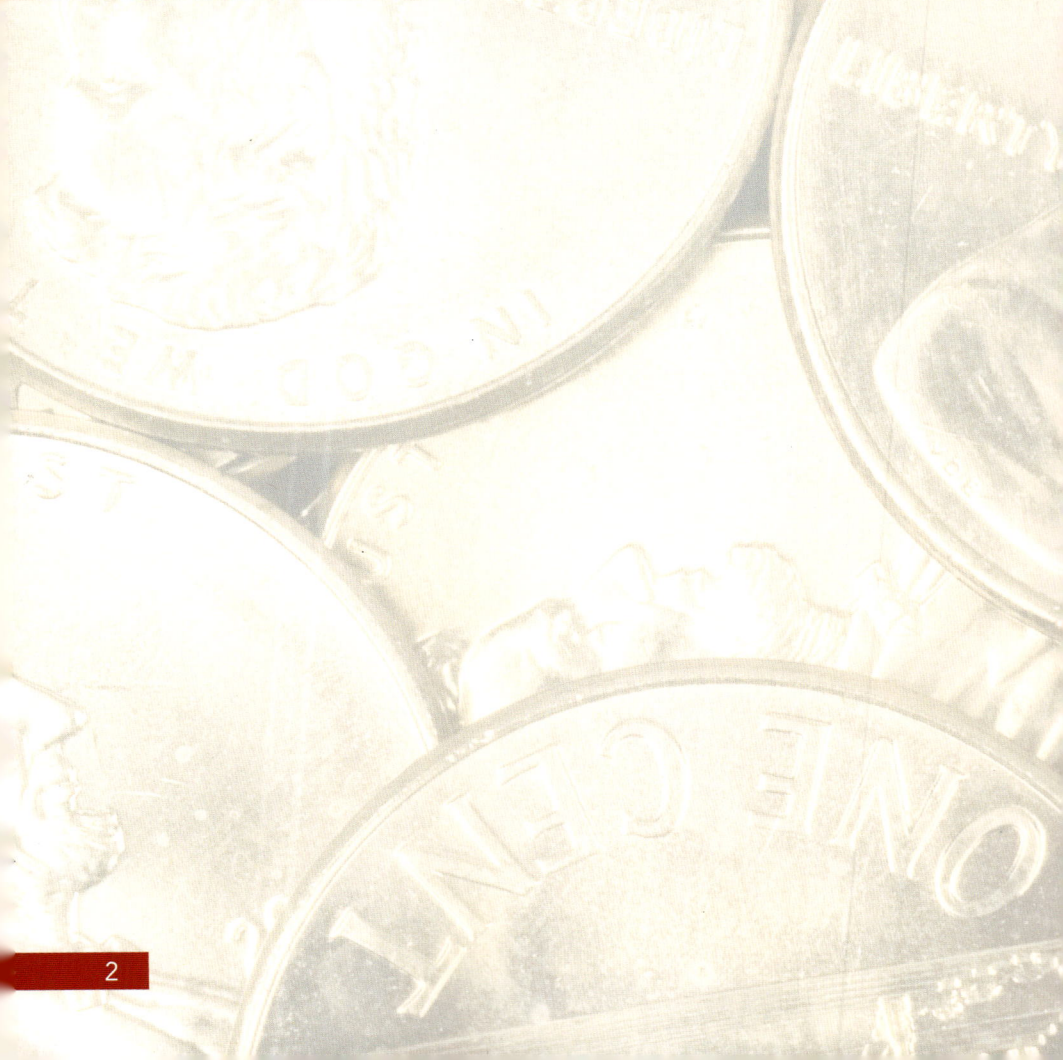

Here is a nickel.
A nickel is 5 cents.

Here is a dime.
A dime is 10 cents.

Here is a quarter.
A quarter is 25 cents.

Here is a dollar.
A dollar is 100 cents.

Here is five dollars.
Five dollars is 500 cents.

Here is ten dollars.
Ten dollars is 1000 cents.

GLOSSARY

penny

nickel

dime

quarter

one dollar

five dollars

ten dollars